Poetic Persuasion:
The Young Carer's Ink

POETIC PERSUASION: THE YOUNG CARER'S INK

First edition. May 1, 2023.

Written by Emmanuel Borges-Da-Silva.
Illustrated by Michael Owusu-Kyereh.

Preface

"In this book, Emmanuel paints vivid imagery that draws you into a journey through grief and joy, disappointment and hope, insecurities, relationships and life transitions. He writes from a raw and vulnerable place, as one who has travelled this road and not just as a casual observer. Most importantly, he writes as one who has travelled the road with God and is a testimony of God's power to preserve us through life's most difficult experiences. Read this book, be comforted, be challenged and receive hope."
~ Daniel Ogbonna, Poet.

"A deeply moving body of work to visit and revisit. Get a box of tissues ready as Eman unfurls his thoughts and heart."
~ Pẹlúmi, author of *Love LETTERS & HEART Ramblings*

"Emmanuel's tender portrait of love, faith and hope is honest and revelatory"
~ Lanaire Aderemi, *bless the memory*

Foreword

Emmanuel takes us into the place called deep. A depth that is only reached when you choose to go deep. This book is a deep calleth unto deep kind of read. The first entry 'Child-Parent' captivated me the most, it took me beneath the surface, surpassed my understanding of Eman and brought me into an intimate knowledge of who he really was and what it really was like being a carer of his beloved mother. If you thought you knew Emmanuel, these writings will bring you into a new dimension of who he is, of how you see him. The God Letters are a sacred gift, something that I personally believe Emmanuel was created, fashioned and ordained to grace the world with.

This book is beautiful, not because it's all nice stories, but because it's redemptive of seeing all things working together for good, and God making everything beautiful in its time. That time is now.

Moreover, we see tapestry of God's faithfulness, love and wisdom being brewed through each entry in this book. We see a mirror of Jesus grew in wisdom and stature, Emmanuel's writing give us his pearl of wisdom given by God and we witness his stature of a young boy into a mature man. This book will inspire, heal and empower you.

Emmanuel, you never fail to amaze me with your uniqueness, surely this book places you into the hallways of greats who penned their life, that a generation would recount and testify of the faithfulness and miraculous power of God.

Proud of you, all my love, PA.

-

Ayokunu Oduniyi
Creative & Corporate Photographer
Leader of A New Thing London & 4:12 Men

"I am squeezed, ink I leak.
Thrown to and fro by the tremors of life,
I spill ink.
I can't help but write about it all,
as if the pen was holding me to ransom.
Love, manhood, pain, purpose...
Come and learn
from the ink blots of a young carer
who has seen valleys and built castles there;
castles that remain."

Get your heart ready.

Table of Contents

In loving memory of our loved ones who have passed on.

This is for all the young carers, the minorities, the sceptics, the doubters, the hopeless, the depressed, the lovers, and those who have known pain, grief and injustice.

Be poetically persuaded to change your perspective for the better.

I: Innocence

Child-Parent

Take me quietly to the womb and bring me back my
umbilical cord; where I hear my mother's heartbeat
and embrace my daily feed.
For I am playing God... usurping a position that does
not belong to me. My biology will not stretch. I am a
child-parent, but a child nonetheless.

I am a child parent
Parenting a parent child
I am my parent's child
I did not chase manhood
Manhood chased me down in the wild.
Childhood is the future for us.
The future is now.
I want to grow back down.

Glass Shoulders

I have strong glass shoulders
On one hand,
I have dislocated them on three instances
On the other hand,
They have carried responsibility over distances
A pack mule
Carrying a home, others' disabilities and school
Auto-pilot was my best friend
Until my shoulders broke
My mind snapped
Atlas met his end.
I couldn't carry the world anymore

I finally realised
That there is nothing strong about my glass
shoulders
Nothing bold about carrying heavy loads
So I crawled into weakness' embrace
I asked for help
... *It was the strongest thing I ever did.*

School Days

I was a bullied bully

This is how it went in school—
Insults wrapped in banter
Hurt wrapped in laughter
Lies wrapped in compliments thereafter
Our words put holes in hearts
                    I see some of them these days...
                    From the cages of our palaver;
                    Some escaped
        But most became exactly what we would say
                    "Dumb"
                    "Pussy"
                    "Wasteman"
                    "Ugly"
                    "Butters"
                    "Hoe"
                    "Slag"
            Our words moulded their homes

....

Now we know better
So if what you're about to say is not more
beautiful than silence
Stay silent
Or expand your vocabulary
We don't need any more self-fulfilled prophecies

Innocence

Innocence, so lost but so important
True internal wealth that lays dormant
The treasure that we are all trying to find
                Innocence
                I no sense... I used to have no sense
                of evil
Skin colour used to be beautiful expression
A different way to see the world and hear God's
voice through many accents
Opposite gender used to be "lurgies" and not
immorality
                Opposite gender used to be purity
My eyes used to see no evil
Girls used to be human beings
Ethnicity used to be like all purpose seasoning
Giving flavour and new taste to my infant palette

Oh how the adventure in my mind would wreak
havoc
High as trees, we would swing on monkey bars
Low as muddy ground, we would crawl on grassy
fields
The stains on our clothes would be our trophies
Not the mortgage or the positions we apply for
to impress people that don't care about us
                A simpler time
Before bills and oppression-induced stress
That lead to taking pills to substitute innocent
zest

Relevance, the Not-so-friendly Ghost

Everyone my age is *"making moves"*... But moving
nowhere fast
Chasing the elusive phantom called relevance
A ghost conjured up by other people... not God
Zombies aimlessly hungering for something that
won't satisfy them
What happened to having hobbies that weren't
about making money?
What happened to talking on the phone to laugh
and to build up.. not gossip about others in the
dark?

Why do you perform for those who don't care about you?

You don't have to... you know that, right?

Acting "Grown"

When did we become so internally old
The voice of innocence is numb
When did our hearts grow wax cold?

Why are you trying to grow up so quickly
Don't you know that it's a trap
A door that leads to empty empires
You will grow tired
Of acting "grown up" in front of others who
regurgitate and redigest their own insecurities on
a daily basis
So, who are they to tell you to be stiff and less
childlike? Enjoy life

Acting grown and being mature are two different
things
Maturity is internal and external management
Acting grown is fighting your innocent
undertones
Because you want to be boxed into a fake
corporate mould

Starving Children

Being a child is a mindset
One that we have allowed to slip into the abyss
They say that your spirit doesn't age, but it's your
soul that picks up taint
Like a clean shoe in mud
soles pick up taint
Greed and pride, adult qualities in this world that
are not serving you and I
I wish they would band together and fly,
Off into the night like the moon's disappearing
magic trick when we see the sunrise
We don't need them
They only fuel the egos in our heads
But leave the children on the insides of us
begging for bread

Begging to run

Begging to love

Begging to fly

Begging to cry

Begging to connect with the ones that we were
taught by society to marginalise

Begging to play... with those who you have been
taught to hate.

There's Another

"I believe that this neglected, wounded,
inner child of the past is the major source
of human misery." ~ John Bradshaw

There's another who sits in you.
I can see past the exterior decor
Past the walls of Jericho you maintain
Inside
There is a being who fights to grasp the light
A neglected child surrounded by the dark
Every time you open up
Another leaves.
Many don't stop to bother unless you're the final
product.

Let me introduce myself
I am a steadfast support
More reliable than a crutch
My eyes see reality,
the fragile child locked within your entity
I am closer than the darkness
Brighter than the light you are chasing
I am Love
Eyes of a dove
True love
The kind of love that will take nails to the hand
I am real love. You don't deserve any less.

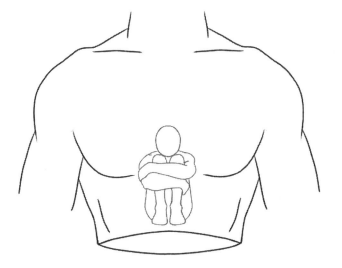

The Balloon of Yesterday

Young carer
How many nights have you spent
Staring into the night sky hoping to be rescued
Endless days you've wanted to fly away
And catch childhood by its tail
Childhood, the balloon of yesterday
Endless days you've wanted to fly away...

Young carer has never really been young
Young carers are parents
Parents pastoring parents
Pupils playing principals
... You became a man of the house, before a
man...
Shazam!
In an instant, you were no longer a child
You were statically shocked suddenly like
lightning
As your guardian became a dependent
Childhood flunked class
And was marked absent

Whilst they played the role;
"I'll be mummy" and "I'll be
daddy" with baby dolls,

we became.

Dad is a human

"When you're young, you think your dad is Superman. Then you grow up, and you realise he's just a regular guy who wears a cape."

~ Anonymous

I used to hate my dad.

I assumed that his absence was his rejection. It was less to do with me, more to do with him. When I was young I had a picture, a picture that had no blemish. "That's what a father was supposed to look like", I said to myself. Never failing. Perfect. Never changing up.

Almost like God.

Which now doesn't make sense. I took his absence personally, as if I was his idol, or at the centre of his decision making. I never once thought about him.

Maybe Dad was hurting.

I was given a title once. It was when God called me His child. A title that did not represent what I do. A title I couldn't always live up to, even today. Being a dad must be the same. A title you can never fully live up to, only try to live up to. I'm sure my dad still looks in the mirror, readjusting all of his insecurities... Just like me. I'm certain that he still has to look himself dead in the eye and give himself the grace others are too "perfect" to give him.

No one is perfect. Everyone needs grace.

Your dad may have been present but emotionally
absent. Your dad may have been a shadow,
known of, but never held, never touched, a
phantom that rivalled water vapour. You may not
love the title, but forgive the human because
whether you like it or not, he is present
whenever you look in the mirror, in your
appearance and your own imperfections.
I forgot that Dad was a human before he was
Dad.

Dad is a human before he is dad
and I love him.

II: Decay & Hope

Miss Doubtfire

She is, trials, hardship | She is everything I hate
in this world | She is every obstacle and loss I've
ever had the pleasure of meeting | She is the
death of my brother | She is the disability of my
mother | She is a house burnt down | She is
unrequested responsibility at a young age | She is
the absence of a father figure | She is heartbreak |
She is depression

But without her fiery form which burns my
hands at the touch... I would never know what I
truly love

Without her I would never know what true value
is...
I would have never discovered how beautiful the
pieces of myself are **that she can never burn**

Sometimes,
fire burns away everything you adore
to show you that there is more at your core...
Child,
you are chastised consistently so that your
corrupted corpse may call out to its calling

What chaotic choreography
Behold her rough routines

Fire can cook or destroy
Fire can mould or burn
Fire can refine or scorch
Same with hardships

Is it consuming you?
Or is it making you everything
you have been longing to be?

Nuclear Fission

Divorce is never the end
Because every time ex-partners cross paths or
dot eyes
they die again

Divorce is a perpetual death
It goes on and on and on and on
Like the fear of marriage it evokes

It goes on and on and on and on
Like a waterfall of pain
It goes on and on and on and on

Not just for the couple
but for daughters and sons
Divorce is the splitting of atoms
Two souls were once one whole
Now radiation is mutating the home

Which leaves the children
Imitating gymnasts
Split in two as their minds try to configure who
to side with

Dark Tunnel

*"The broken will always be able to love
harder than most because once you've
been in the dark, you learn to appreciate
everything that shines." ~ Anonymous*

Sometimes depression is a tunnel
With a light teasingly being dangled,
Close enough to keep me going,
But too far to reach.   *I am an anglerfish*
Sometimes depression is my mind going
mercenary establishing its own truth
False truth.
A grumpy toddler, you can't change its mind
Even I can't in those times

...

"God, do you hate me for a crime I don't recall
committing? Have I served my sentence? Has
your bail of mercy been processed yet? Have you
syphoned enough hope from me? Am I ready for
rebirth? To rise with humility? Is the humbling
coming to an end? ~~Do you even see me~~?"

Am I blaming the only One who can save me?

Prize Draw

Will you get lost again in your feelings?
Into the labyrinth
The maze of emotions
Full of haze because you don't know what you'll
get today
Will you get laughter and joy as you thank God
for the little things?
Or will you get a fall, head burst open, with
blood on the floor?
How will disability address our young carer
today?
Maybe you'll see your mother cry again
And her tears will be ink and her expressions a
pen
As her lamentations are inscribed into your heart
As if they were the word of God

As she regrets having children because of the
condition that plagued your late brother
That she did not create but carries....

What will the young carer win today?
I pray that it's a cruise to the island of laughter
and joy
The other prizes seem hard to avoid

A House on Fire

The potent smell of burning plaster

The piercing sound of the smoke alarm

The grace of being awake

The preservation of a mum who's disabled

I lost *everything* and *nothing* at the same time

My house was on fire

But our souls still untouched

What a miracle

Decay

I didn't know pain
True pain
Until I saw my brother begin to decay
                Emulating a sweet tooth
A wave of degeneration
His muscles were lacking vibrations
But his hands
Though ailing and bone
They seemed
To be full of gratitude
His hands desired life more than my own
What would he say about us?

my mind wanders...

If my brother's hands could enunciate

> *... WE must love our lots in life,*
> *this onion-resemblant timeline;*
> *for it is a layered*
> *gift that the dead are*
> *disqualified from unwrapping.*

Look at you brother

You're still teaching me from the grave

He Wept

With an offering plate full of mourning
He sat in service
And he wept:

"I CAN'T DO THIS ANYMORE!"

... his spirit became empty,
he was poor,
lacking in reason to live,
needy to the core,
but this cry,
cast out devils,
initiated resurrection,
this weakness opened him to perfection.

It's time to cry.
release the dams.
open the floodgates.
you don't have to drown anymore.
there is a reservoir in heaven asking for
donations.

FOMO

DICTIONARY DEFINITIONS

FOMO or **fo·mo** [**foh**-moh]

Slang.

a feeling of anxiety or insecurity over the possibility of missing out on something, as an event or an opportunity: fear of missing out.

E.g. My friend Ebenezer has serious **FOMO** when the group meetup is getting fun. He may even turn his car back around to stay for longer. Pray for him.

Young Caring [yuhng ˈkɛːrɪŋ]

a feeling of anxiety or insecurity over the possibility of missing out on something, as an event or an opportunity: fear of missing out.

E.g. On some days, you could have a chance to be a normal kid, doing normal things with normal people. Until your phone rings like a tag, you were just on probation. Day carer says "Your brother isn't feeling well today and you need to be home early to take care of him". It's hard to catch up with people when you've grown up missing out. FOMO is synonymous with young caring.

Ask for help.

This is your sign.

Maybe this time, it won't
amount to nothing.

Again, I plead.

Ask for help.

Break the cycle in your family, disrupt the culture of closed lips.

Ask for help.

This is your last call.

Ask for help.

Be the first weak one who gains true strength.

Ask for help

Anxiety

You're a squatter in the heart
You treat the present like the plague
So scared of focusing on today
Worry personified
The amalgamation of perceived bad outcomes
    and failure unseen
The opposite of faith
The substance of thoughts self-sabotaging in
nature
And the evidence of the fear of things not yet
seen
Present pleasure?
Contentment?
Not in your dictionary
You're the kind of person to destroy your own
home
You seem not to care about the mental state you
bring on your host

...

You're also a liar
Telling me of a bad future that even you have no
clue about
And silly me
90 percent of the time I listen
But now I'm on a mission
I'm going to take the 10 percent now
Let the 90 percent go missing
My ears are closed for good
You are banned
This is the end of your *present* stealing plans

Because today is a *gift*
One that I don't often get to enjoy in your midst
Anxiety... I evict you
I'm enjoying today.

Rubik's Cube

Hurt people,   *hurt* people
I gave my heart   fully once
It was treated like a rubik's cube that you get
tired of playing with
Thrown to the side; bin collection on Friday
morning.
Funny thing is

                    I'm not even scared of giving
                              it away again...

I'm scared that I'll be the new frustrated rubik's
cube player with her heart..
The future girl whom I will love
Whoever she is
I'm scared that my inner man
Is still holding onto past pain
And is ready to give that pain from the past
To a present innocent bystander
The new girl that's taken my breath away
Whoever she is

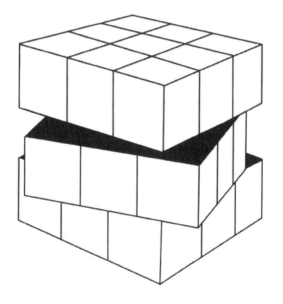

Heaven's Butterfly

The Counsellor:
"Death is kinda beautiful
I don't mean to be morbid
But if a caterpillar never sheds and *spreads* its skin
We would never see this *butter*(fly)
The caterpillar dies, the butterfly flies
So why are you so scared of death to self?
If you never die to self on this Earth
Heaven can never give you wings"

Escape/Ascension

I am, I was, a broken thing
Longing to escape.
Now I long to live.
And sometimes, being awake isn't enough
anymore
I long to be *truly* awake
Outside of this body one day
Truly His
Truly free,
When I die
Or when He comes for me

Hey Depression

*"I was so scared to give up depression,
fearing that somehow the worst part of
me was actually all of me. " ~ Elizabeth
Wurtzel*

When we hit rock bottom
Trumpets of glory sound real quiet
The echo of silence becomes life's soundtrack
A deep silence
Then island
Alone, on the shores of your own fearful
imaginations

These are the birth pains before Depression
announces himself
He's a multilayered beast, an amalgamation of
muffled emotions all trying to have their say at
the same time.
Like crabs in a barrel
Loneliness does not respect apathy

The shouting match continues

But if you close your eyes long enough and
depress Depression by feeding Hope with your
favourite pastime, you can overcome him
Eventually

He is loud. Loud because he is scared
Depression is on a timer,
And when you pay him no attention, he gets
violent
It's a sign that you're losing the tyrant

Hey Depression
We won't miss you

The Dancing Leaf

My mum is a single leaf
Frail and flimsy
But trusting in the wind
to move her to where she needs to go
Also full of revelation and beauty for those who
slow down to watch her dance in this wind.
My mum is a single leaf
Frail and flimsy
Trusting that the wind of God
will take her to where she needs to go
For she cannot go there on her own
My mum is a single leaf
But owns more peace than you and me

The Arms of Doubt

It was *there*
I felt comforted

In *her* arms
I felt most secure

Because in *her* arms,
I could be everything
that I wanted to be

and everything that I didn't want
to remain as.

Her name is Doubt, and she is *painfully* alluring.

Words of a Passerby

Hope and heartbreak can coexist in the mouth of
a stranger
In the mouth of a passerby were words that
caused the mystery reaction

Hope and heartbreak

"Are you Anthony's brother?"
She says with cheerful and familiar eyes
"Yes I am, I guess we resemble each other"

"How is he?"
She seemed elated

"He passed away"
I stated

The atmosphere changed
My words were global warming as her eyes
became polar ice caps that were on the brink of
melting point.

For a brief second... She was mourning too
As if we were playing hopscotch with grief
"Wow, ~~he was~~ such a *good* boy. And how's mum?"

Do you see it?
Hope and heartbreak

She must've known him when the condition was
in effect
I'm sure she could tell the tales of how his frail
body danced a dance of joy that this world had
never seen

How his smile was a silent gospel choir lifting
spirits...

She knew me, but I had no clue who she was.
There was just familiarity

> *You begin to discard faces that grief does not*
> *encourage you to keep*—convinced that there are
> better things to be kept close to your heart,
> valuable enough to make an abode in your
> long-term memory stores;

Basketball at Rowan Park.
Regretful arguments
Out of key duets to John Legend
Payback

Hope and heartbreak can coexist in the mouth of
a stranger
In the mouth of a passerby were words that
caused the mystery reaction

Hope and heartbreak
I began to remember

Through the Eyes of The Seed

"A seed neither fears light nor darkness,
but uses both to grow." ~ Matshona
Dhliwayo

How does one
find comfort in darkness?
Friend... I know. It seems like you
haven't seen sunlight in days; a darkness so close,
walls so near, claustrophobia sets in. It's because
you are a seed friend. But one day, you will stand
tall and see over distances that the darkness
could've never helped you to imagine. So here's
your comfort for the day: You're growing, and
many others will hide under your shade, birds
will make nests on your branches, and those in
need of you will eat your fruits. So right now,
begin to shadow box. Mustard seed,
begin to act like a mustard tree, rooted and
grounded in the comfort that hope brings.
You are amazing... They just don't
know it yet.

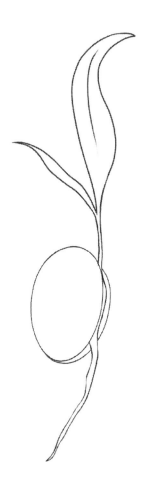

An Answered Prayer

Young caring, an *adventure* and a *nightmare*

An *adventure*
                    where you learn what
                selfless love looks like in real time
A *nightmare*
                where the fear of premature death
                follows you like your own shadow

A young carer's biggest fear is that their care is
not enough to sustain their guardians
But you must remember, it was never your job to
sustain life
Neither does your human frame possess the
power in itself to do so

Leave the higher things to the Higher One
And be grateful for each day as it comes
because nothing is promised but eternal life for
those who believe
So don't concede
Don't give up

God sees your labour of love.

Young carer, don't forget who you are
You are a gift from heaven wrapped in human flesh
An answered prayer of anguish for your guardians
Your life and impact is bigger than the
experiences you missed out on
You're a miracle

More than a young carer
And if the world doesn't see it, just know I do

I said into the mirror

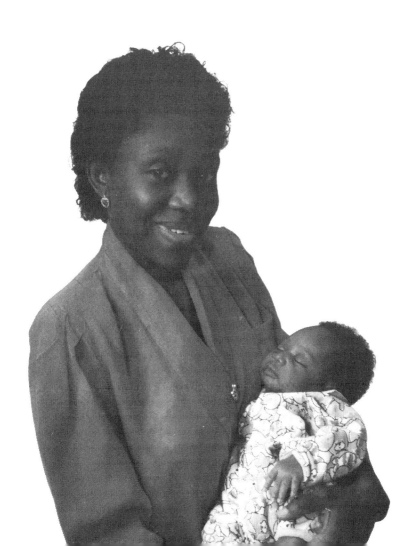

III: Shimmer of Love

One Step Is Everything

*"One small step for man, one giant leap
for mankind" ~ Neil Armstrong*

A bit out of context, but Neil Armstrong had a
good point
Your small steps forward are shifting the course
of your whole life
It may seem like a small step for you, but it takes
bravery to move
It's easy to remain stagnant
It's easy to let circumstances make executive
decisions for you

So if no one will tell you, I most certainly will
Friend, every step you take is a milestone
Every time you choose to stare grief in the face
the angels clap for you
Life is a marathon and not a race

Run at your own pace
You are never behind, everything can change in
the blink of an eye
One conversation, one opportunity, one
application
So you keep trotting, even with your limp
Your limp will always be beautiful to me
And your *limp* will always be a *run* to an onlooker

Were you ever limping in the first place?

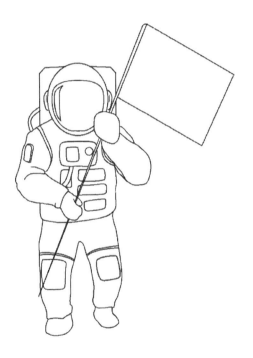

Mind Masseuse

She greets me with a smile

"Welcome home friend!" she exclaims.
"Let me take your coat, oh, and your bag too.
Take off your drenched hat and hit the sack. It's
always raining outside these days, you don't get
too many breaks. But I've reserved this time just
for you. Lay your head down on my massage
table. Today, let my words be like a masseuse to
your mind. Let's bring balance back to your
brain. You're doing so much better than you give
yourself credit for. Living, adulting, is a skill that
very few, if anyone, has mastered. ***Grass always
looks greener when it's artificial.***

So,
> Let's unravel that knot of comparison.

> The grass is *never* truly greener."

Would you really be happy if
you had their life?
Okay, now you've got it. What
next?
... and what after that?

-

You will never be truly joyful
until you settle your heart in
something long-lasting,
something eternal.

My Fireplace

Ever been comforted by a mere look?

In every period of my frantic life
There has always been someone I can look at
To be filled with encouragement deep inside

You keep finding me

In the form of a brother, sister, mother.
Or a lover
In your eyes, I find all the comfort I need
Your lens, a place of perspective
Your iris, a fireplace with silence
Your pupil, where I see my self-worth

Keep finding me

Show up in any form you wish
Because in your eyes
I'm actually valuable

Tears in a Bottle

"You keep track of all my sorrows. You have collected all my tears in Your bottle. You have recorded each one in Your book."~ Psalms 56:8

The Gardener. He seems troubled. Concerned.

The Gardener:

> "It was raining today. I was trying to water the garden
> Fill My earth with droplets of growth. I always finish what I started
> So how much more you?
>
> Just as you catch the rain in the palm of your hands
> I catch your tears before they land
> ... *Your tears*
> I catch them before they land.
> In my bottle they stay
> And I keep them for a rainy day
> So don't hide your tears away.
> No, don't hide your tears away
> Because in this bottle
> Your tears are a reminder for me to act on your behalf.
> *Everytime a tear drops it moves my heart*
> So have faith
> I'm not far away".

You Aren't Good Enough

"You alone are enough. You have nothing to prove to anybody." ~ Maya Angelou

Yes
You aren't good enough
Yes
You'll never be good enough for them
And that's okay
At the end of the day
They aren't good enough for themselves
They hang their own flaws on the shelves
For all to see
They are hypocrites indeed

So is anyone good enough?

Stop trying to be good enough
Just be
That's enough

Adornment

You used to feel comfortable wearing nothing
    (That's not what I mean) Hear me out
Before you took on labels
Adornment was a foreign thing
           (the same way they stared at this black man
               on the streets of Chania in Crete, Greece)

A foreign thing
Having to dress yourself in the opinions of
others
Was out of sight and out of mind
Until you thought you needed them

The scary thing about adornment
Is that you don't know where it came from:
      Whether you are still dressing up for old
      lovers
      Or new ones that you are scared will
      discover
                    who you really are

    Friend, if you have to be adorned to be loved
        They weren't for you in the first place

Love Is Blind

"If love is blind, then maybe a blind person that loves
has a greater understanding of it." ~ Criss Jami

My mum
My mum can't see
Not even pixelated pictures cross her vision
She sees the colour of tarmac
Her image of me is a contract
Her eyes signed on the dotted line
A legal bind to be blind
In fact
Her son has been amiss for quite some time
But she still knows me
Still sees my needs
Above her own
Her love won't leave me alone

Who is it that blindly loves you?

Keep them close and let them know how much you value them.

Love Speaks

What is love?
        Love is hard
        Love is more than roses and chocolates
        Love is patient. Love is kind. Love bears
        no grudges
        Love never stops giving
        Love is beautiful, and so love is taken
        advantage of by *ugly people*

           Like my kind brothers, who are left for
                men who treat women like slaves

           Love is gentle, so love is abused and *beaten black and blue*

           Like my sisters, who are physically and
                emotionally abused daily by *weak men*

           Love is me and love is you

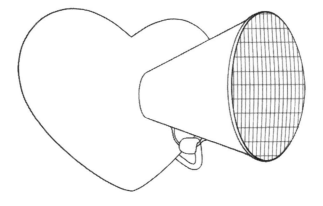

When I Say Love

"Love is patient, love is kind. It does not envy, it does not boast, it is not proud. It does not dishonour others, it is not self-seeking, it is not easily angered, it keeps no record of wrongs. Love does not delight in evil but rejoices with the truth. It always protects, always trusts, always hopes, always perseveres." ~ 1 Corinthians 13:4-7

When I say love
I instantly think of romance
I don't think about mercy and kindness

When I say love
I think about butterflies in the belly
I don't think about the homeless man's belly or
whether he is hungry

When I say love
I think about Valentine's Day
I don't think about sacrifice or agape

When I say love...
Do I really know what I'm saying?

Monkey with a Gun

As I walk through memory banks of intimacy
I relive moments of transparency
I pick up pieces of my soul along the shores of
heartbreak
And I say to myself:

"*Never again*. Never again will I let you hold my
heart. Like a monkey who's been given a gun,
you were trigger happy with the transparent
ammunition I gave you. But without surrender,
true love is unattainable. What a risky, and
rewarding game love is."

Mother Nature

I want you to be my new habitat.
You're a work of art,
You're more beautiful than a symphony by Mozart.
I've stared at your face enough times now to
conclude
*That you might just be an amalgamation of all things
beautiful.*
You are unmatched. You are undisputed.

*If they could name the sunsets in Nairobi they would
name them after you,*
Golden child
*Word on the grapevine is that Mother Nature is full of
jealousy. Why?*
She gets the silent treatment from us
When you walk into the room.
Because I'd rather hear you speak
Than watch the waves crash against the shore.
I'd rather stare into your boundless brown eyes
*Than watch the expansion of space and the stars in the
sky.*

The Engineer

Dear Crush,

You're always working hard,
Sometimes I think too hard
More mileage than a used car
But more horsepower than a Bugatti
One day,
I'd love to be able to provide a massage MOT for
your feet
Repairs for your tense and hardworking
shoulders
Topped off with a car wash
Sweet compliments of truth
Oil, from the lips of this engineer
Lavished on you

From, The Engineer.

Offspring of Divorce

Marriage,
A divine harmony that pierces hearts,
A love that doesn't stop and start
Your love is continuous
Through mountains and valleys
Through rocky shores and tall oak trees
Through sickness and health
Through poverty and wealth
I wish this is what I witnessed
I wish divorce didn't affect everyone

This void must be fed
This vacancy in the eyes of my upbringing
May love fill it for all of us,
the offspring of divorce.

Just Love

I once asked a friend

What
If
Love
Isn't
About
You?

Would it still be appealing?

His heart flared up
His true colours rose to the surface
He said

If I can't receive
then why should I give?

Is it really love
if you're waiting
on a condition?
If everyone
just loved...
Then...

Stop complaining about a lack of love that *you don't show*

You can complain, or you can be the change

A Mother's Love

There is a love you don't play with
A mother's love
You play with that
You play with your life
You may even pay with your life

Her children are more precious to her
Than silver or gold
Than riches untold
It is a mystery how love
Can turn a mother into a warrior
In the blink of an eye

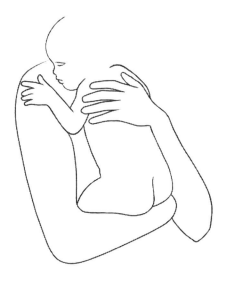

Honey

*"And the man and his wife were both
naked and were not ashamed." ~ Genesis
2:25*

Just like honey is always sweet
May our love never lack in taste
When we get married
May honeymoon become honeysun
Love, you have permission to speak for us all day
long
Dawn to setting
Honeymoon become honeysun
Love lead all day long

Fear of Confession

Scared that our friendship will crumble

//

If I find anyone after you

//

I will always be settling

//

"Did I settle for the wrong selection?"

//

This is the fear of confession

Sacrosanct

If I was on Love's PR & Marketing Team, I would
write to the press:

Love is sacrosanct.

*It is not to be played with by boys who don't know how
to strum it correctly.*

Love is sacred.

Not to be received by girls who don't see it's value.

Love is neither left nor right, male nor female,
slave nor free.

Love is
                                    So holy, set apart.
Love
Is not always like us
It calls us higher
and still gives to those who are undeserving
and still continues to act the same after rejection.

Love is the ultimate philanthropist,
because love does not seek notoriety,
not tainted by responses or the opinions of
people.
Love will not stop giving if giving becomes
politically incorrect.
                                    Love is what it is.
Will never change or buckle, sway or be
uprooted.

Love is sacrosanct.

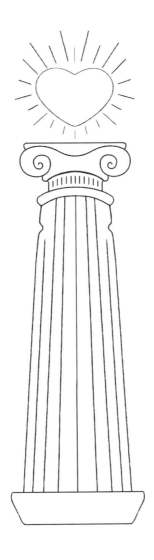

Embrace Uncomfortable

You are worth a love that is "too much"
A love that makes you feel uncomfortable
A love that wages wars on your insecurities
A love that destroys the "I'm not good enough"
that bellows from your soul

True love is uncomfortable

I made a discovery about love.

When it is unbelievable,
It is most real.

Nakama

On my 25th birthday.
Humans flocked like birds, as if escaping a storm
that was about to hit
to the fields of green and scorching hot sun.
The heatwave wouldn't stop us from having fun.

"IT'S TIME FOR A SPORTS DAY!"
We ran, we competed, things got a little heated.
The usual.
As I lay on the grass with a pulled hamstring
A thought came to my mind that my heart would
be the one to bring:
"I wonder why they gathered?"

Sometimes my heart can't fathom that they love
me.

(The jollof rice I provided can be eaten at home,
it's not special.)

Birds migrate when they sense *danger* or sense
opportunity.
Either way, people flock around us for a sense of
immunity or *unity.*
It is an honour that you are seen as an oasis away
from storms.
We gather around campfires because they keep
us warm.

Next time you are questioning who you are,
Remember the friends who hold your heart, who
cover your scars.
Real wealth
They will see more in you than you'll ever see in
yourself

They are God's reminder to you that you are
valuable,
You are more than palatable.
You are sought after.

For every person born, someone receives a gift
they never asked for.
You are one of those gifts.
Maybe God cries;
Two reasons of sorrow and joy come to mind:
One, We leave Him for a short time; sorrow.
Two, when we are born,
He knows that other migrants will find us as they
avoid the storm; joy.

And we too will find them.
I love my friends.

IIII: I Won't Forget You...

Ode to Jimmy Rogers

*"It's not about winning the game of basketball.
It's about winning the game of life." ~ Jimmy
Rogers*

Basketball training?
More like *athletics*
Oh, we would run!
As if mad dogs were right on our tails
Then lactic acid would kick in
Our legs would begin to fail
But it was beautiful
As we would hear Jimmy shout
"Drive the body!"
All-Might, Plus Ultra vibes—We were surpassing
our limits
Lactic acid was Goliath

He hated our slingshots, *our persistence*

....

Lactic acid isn't just in sport
He is in your mind
Warning you to stop
A stiff boundary scared of stretching
Don't listen to him!
For whenever you feel resistance, limitations or
pain
Skin is shedding, making you new again
Keep going, keep growing.

In memory of Jimmy Rogers, the greatest
basketball coach I ever had. I guess there was a
method to the madness after all.

Ode to Anthony

My head is in the past
Regrettable
As if I were memory-intolerant

I wish my mind were forgetful

Digesting these old picture tapes...
It hurts to remember, to recount the chapters of
insults, strife and malice
The love was brighter than the times of
indifference, most definitely, but I guess Pain has
a stronger adhesive at his disposal
I try to rip away the bad memories, but they take
some pieces with them. Strong adhesive leaves
marks behind taking the pink lining of my mind
with it
I am grateful for the glimmers of love we shared.
My brother, our beauty, our bonding times, they
are more potent than pain's punches

—---

I wasn't there when you passed
When you were gasping for air, full of despair
and fear
I was nowhere
Oh how I wished to have offered a hand for you
to squeeze!
Or offered encouraging words on bent knees!
Brother, I know
It's not something I could've controlled
And I know you're smiling from above the dome

So brother, now all I have is this hope
That when I see you I will tell you about how
inspiring you are
*I will tell you 1000 times until it breaks through your
glorified skin*
Until words of affirmation sink in like light
through cracked wall
Like the colour brown becoming a part of leaf
colours in the fall...

In the presence of the angels
I will hold your face
I will stare into your eyes, brother
And I will say

> *"I missed you,*
> *so very much*
> *Let us dance,*
> *like two stringed instruments in harmony,*
> *like two submitted servants pleased to wash each*
> *other's feet,*
> *like brothers,*
> *like brothers,*
> *who deeply love each other"*

Until then, keep the clouds warm for me,
And keep singing to God with the stars,
And keep dancing with all your heart
Because you can now, truly, freely
I can't wait to see you again
I lost my brother, but he found peace

Ode to Abigail

"For as a man thinks within himself, so is he." ~ Proverbs 23:7

There's this girl
She reminds me of my mum
Her name's Abigail
Bubbly, like a glass of champagne
Smile, like a ray of sunshine
And laughter that somehow overwrites any disaster
There was no way you would know that she had epilepsy and a brain tumour
Unless she told you herself

Abigail taught me the difference between riches and true wealth
Wealth is not just health:
wealth is what you think about yourself

So, what do I think about myself?
Even when my body starts to fail or I begin to lose my own mind...
Will I still find comfort in being alive?
Will the edges of my smile be corners where people can gather and hope again?
Or will I refuse to choose comfort and continue to be addicted to pain?

I want to be like Abigail.
I want to see my pain as an afterthought and my joy at the forefront
Because watching Abigail, through pain, smile somehow, made life worth living again.
So, reader and friend,
Don't believe the lie.

Abigail chose and found comfort in such hard times.
She inspires me—
And I hope she inspires you too.

Ode to Luna

The moon mimics you, my precious niece.
For when the sun went dim and life was dull, you
stole our hearts and lit up the dark

I'm sure your parents would testify to your
fireworks...
It still hurts.
You were 6 months old when you were called
back home.

The moon,
It shines for a short time, pictures are taken to
make it last longer than a lifetime
A glimpse of your innocent face was more
valuable than a lifeline.

If the moon—which mostly appears at night—is
seen as valuable then how much more you?
So many people your life brought value to.

God knew you before the moon.
Luna, the moon, was named after you.

Rest in peace my beautiful niece.

Ode to Chris

Older siblings are many things...
Our relationships with them... many things.

annoying, bullish and power trippy

but the most faithful when it comes down to it.

Older siblings are parents, 2.0.

Especially older brothers.

To be an older brother is to be replicated—to be
the primary pattern post-parents that your
sub-siblings subconsciously mould themselves
into.

But... to be MY older brother is to be superman,
seemingly bulletproof to trauma,
a comforter,
a disciplinarian,
a disciple,
a forerunner,
a father

To be Chris is to fight against all odds and still
come out on top.
To be Chris is to be a young carer, academic
achiever, faith-filled fighter, dutiful doctor and
the original poetic persuader.
To be Chris is to surpass everything that I could
have ever wanted in an older brother.

I am convinced that God partners with older
siblings to show us that he really does give us

exceedingly and abundantly more than we could ever ask, think or imagine.

To be an older sibling is to be God's goodness in motion.
To be Chris is to be the greatest older brother I could've ever asked for.

I think you should give your older sibling or older role model a call... now please.

Let them know how valuable they are and have been.

Ode to Nyasha

#1: Pre-decision
If someone were to ask me
"What's your future wife like?"
I would say, firstly,
That's too broad of a question
You have to give me categories

She is a person
A being made up of fractions of experiences
Experienced day by day, minute by minute
Her soul is a universe in earthen vessel
Let alone her spirit which is timeless
I don't have enough time on this side of eternity
to examine her thoroughly
Even her earthen vessel is like good soil
Her eyes, like flowers waiting to blossom

Pop
                    goes my easel because I couldn't
paint her even if I tried,
she's too bright for my dull light of imagination
In between her hips, a portal between heaven
and earth that will birth many nations
More precious than a wall street of gold, she is
the broker between man and God's throne
As God sends His children to Earth for her to
take care of them as her own
And her curves like hills, and her neck like a
valley I want to lay and graze in like a deer
panting for waters
Her words, living waters, wisdom walking
She struts her legs like two towers above the
clouds

She is the King of Kings child

That's just a summary
So please be a bit more specific when you ask me
to describe my future wife

——-------------

#2: The decision
When I spoke about this "good woman" I was
always talking about you.
The type of woman I've always told my peers to
go for.
The diamond in the rough
The fairest of 10,000
The kind of gift that your hands feel unworthy to
unwrap.

It scares me that I will love you more later than I
do now.
And I love you a lot. More than I've loved anyone
in my entire life.
You are the most gentle flower, the most easy to
love.
I wonder what kind of man your gentleness will
mould me into.
Will I grow to look more like Jesus as you show
me my flaws without trying?
Will my repentance be deeper and my speech be
slower, and my listening be quicker?
I think so.
I don't think that someone could make a home
near you and remain the same, when God
Himself is the river that flows from your heart.

I repeat: you are the most gentle flower, the most
easy to love.

And it scares me that I will love you more later
than I do now.

May this be a competition of submission and a
soiree of surrender.
As for me, I vow to always tend to you, my
garden.
To water you and to smell your petals only.
For you, I will be holy,
Set apart. By God's grace at the altar we will state,
"Till death do us part."

<u>V: Masculinity: Ruins & Repairs</u>

Guitar's Lament

Another beginner

You play me as if you're fearful
But you mask it with confidence
Like the hands of those
Who play with
And break the strings
of women
Stained bed linen
But no commitment

Ladies
Don't cast your pearls
To those who know
Nothing about their value

Make him wait.
It will expose his real traits

Absent Father Syndrome

Many men I know
Are still recovering from *absent father syndrome*
You know the one?
The one where you chase women
To validate your masculinity
Because you haven't had the intimate validation
of a father

Intimacy is not synonymous with presence
Whether a father is there or not
Is he really *there* or not?

The Counsellor #1

The Counsellor:
"In the UK, men are three times more likely to
commit suicide than women.
In other words
Men are more likely to die from the inside out
than women.
The outward expression of suicide
Is the accumulation of an internal struggle
                A building, silent killer
Brick by brick, trauma by trauma
Connected with the cement of bitterness
Which hardens, like a cold hardened heart
                A building, silent killer.

So,
Is it really cool not to talk to Me?"

Men don't cry.

Instead.

Men commit suicide.

So maybe.

Men should be allowed to cry.

You're Scared

You're scared
If I hug you tight
Your humanity might show
They bullied that out of you though
That's why you're scared
You don't see brotherly love as pure anymore
You remember *punches*
You see *black eyes*
Violence
You remember fights

You now believe that emotions are separate from
your masculinity
Just because they made you a robot
doesn't mean you are

The Counsellor #2

The Counsellor: "Are you really more of a man
for keeping silent?
Buried in anger, self-doubt and despair,
You are wearing toxic masculinity like a cape
But it's really a noose strangling you everyday.

The ones who think they are strong die.
The ones who think they are weak survive and
also thrive.
The reality is
Everyone is weak,
Every man is flawed   and broken
But it's the only the ones who admit it
Who are fixed and stitched

I tell you the truth...
You will never be more of a man by walking
around with leaking wounds,
Leaving blood on every friend, woman and
blessing that's given to you.

So, is it really cool not to talk to Me?"

The Rush

Adrenaline pumping - Blood rushing - This is
what it must feel like to be a man - No
responsibility weighing me down - Perceptions
of freedom like a noose around my neck - An
escape from true accountability - Wild and
boisterous - May my actions be reckless -
Destroying myself and others in the process -
Men are supposed to be angry - Men are
supposed to have no self control

Right?

Well, at least that's what I was taught -
Observations of men, carved into my mind -
Vicarious experiences that could leave you blind
- The men I have seen -
Were raised by boys who refused to grow up -
So they refused to grow up -
And for a short time I too refused to bloom -

Who was your example?

What example will you be?

The Counsellor #3

The Counsellor: *When was the last time your tears had permission to fly?*
Airspace security should never be this tight.
When was the last time your emotions took a deep breath of fresh air?
I know society doesn't teach you to vocalise your despair
But that's why I'm here.

Male.
Father.
Brother.
Son.
Friend.
Man.
Hu... Man.
Human.

It's okay to cry.
It shouldn't be weird to talk to Me.
Who am I?
I am the Counsellor,
I am a gateway to freedom and healing,
And I wonder how many men have to lose themselves and die
Before it's cool to speak to Me.

Delivery, Deliver Me.

My eyes go window shopping down to my chin
To see if my beard has been delivered yet
In hopes of finding Twitter's approval.
How I crave their shipment, their containers of
affirmation.
I am waiting patiently to become a real man.

Daily I stare at the sunset over the waters.
The fisherman is still late to the dockyard.
The mussels/muscles are in transit, hiding in
their shells,
A faulty standard. The scale is imbalanced.
Social media is an anchor that gives weighted
words,
but cannot carry their own generosity.
They have mastered hypocrisy.

/////

What is a man but a male human being who
comes in all shapes and sizes?
What is society's standard but an amalgamation
of opinions derived from untested places, failed
culture, pain, rejection, pride, lust?
Who am I to break under its fallacies as my
shoulders tear to broaden, the epidermis on my
arms sprawl, and my facial skin gapes to birth a
black jungle?
I am slender, smooth, hair-minimal,
gentle-voiced and beautiful.
With what I have received,
a man I am, a man I will be.

Lonely Man

Loneliness looks like
Fabrications in the mind
More real than the woven fabrics on my back
Negative imaginations of the mind
More real than the clothes on my back

Loneliness is feeling closed in
Stuck in a claustrophobic box with no exits
Caved in
Stuck in the mineshaft of your mind's dark
Landslide

An accumulation of gaslighted times

Loneliness looks like a struggling man
Who disregards every helping hand
But deep down
He wants help
But years ago they stole his ability to yell

Through My Eyes

Through my eyes
I see perversion
Sight's bootleg version
The train that carries women as objects in boxes
Contoured into crates of my lustful imaginations
But my sisters are more than what the guys at
school tried to teach me

CAUTION!
FRAGILE AND EXPENSIVE CONTENTS ARE
IN THESE CRATES!

Some of my sisters are my best mates
And one will be worth all the dates
And one will be worth the wait
And one will raise my kids someday God willing
And when I see the way she handles our clan
This gentleman will become a gentle man

Her Own Skin

"Beauty provokes harassment, the law
says, but it looks through men's eyes when
deciding what provokes it" ~ Naomi Wolf,
The Beauty Myth

Who enjoys a nice late night stroll under the
stars?
Not women
They don't get to enjoy it
Because there are demons lurking
In the form of men whose appetites are
insatiable
Some say
"They shouldn't walk out late if they don't want
to get raped..."
I say
"Men need to change how they see their fellow
mate"
When will a woman's soul feel safe
In the skin
It's wrapped in?

Lust's prison sentence is coming soon
As sure as the morning dew
Safely we will all be able to gaze at the moon
... God hates lust too

If the Ground Could Talk

If the ground could talk
Sections would speak in tremors,
an orchestra of gravel.
The road would say to the pavement (*I*)

tremor

The town sleeps, so let us speak

Hello friend, how was your week?

The week was the same as usual.
The smell of exhaust fumes
and rushing tires in the morning,
to beeping horns after 5pm;
Humans call it "rush hour".
Then stillness at night. What about you?

The week was the same as usual.
The smell of coffee
and rushing legs in the morning,
heavy steps after 5pm;
stillness at night.

tremor

What about Friday and Saturday night?
The streets are usually filled with lights!

Isn't it a beautiful sight?

Ah yes! The weekend,
the heaven that they live for.
So many smiles, and less rushing feet
as they mingle and meet.
They dance, they laugh,
their burdens are cast at last,
but after this moment of bliss
the weekend passes fast.

Any new flavours that you got to try
on Friday night?
All I often get to taste is petrol
and the blood of Russian roulette roadkill.
Sometimes I place bets
just to keep my mind fed.
Pavement, let us switch places,
I would love to join the elated.

...

Liquor and vomit.

Pardon me?

The Friday Night Special.
Still want to switch?
Right, I thought as much.

Sighs I don't know
how you take in the smell
and the taste of such.

When there is no escape

from your current reality,
you adapt to your environment eventually.
Even liquor and vomit can become staple

What was your Friday night highlight?

I saw a drunken girl
swaying in the wind;
she was a blade of grass
praying her roots would stay
anchored to my body.
A lad plucked her from my soil
and into a cab.
He wasn't taking her home.

What about the lad?
What was he like?

Sober and alert as a lighthouse

*the pavement's face became contorted, as if he
was grieving.
He continued, unprompted, as if regurgitating
trauma*

What of all the girls
that are swept as dust
by the broom of boys
in men's bodies who don't embody
"I am my sister's keeper"?
What of all the other pavements
whose eyes bleed at the sight of this madness?

(Maybe the pavement cries because we no longer
do.)

I have never had to wake up in unknown territory.
Now this girl will wake up in unknown territory,
Not to a lighthouse, but a black hole, an empty
cathedral of a man.
The light she saw last night was not salvation,
nor heaven, but a white-washed grave
And I,
I will be a witness again next Friday.

Who is strong?

The one who controls their strength, or the one who makes it known?

Who is strong?

The one who uses their strength to protect, or the one who uses their strength to oppress?

Are you strong?

Leadership

Masculinity is leadership; not a dictatorship

A great leader serves his people, treats everyone as an equal

They are a rare breed now, men who serve from love

Ego and pride: *Scary things*

Ego and pride: *Scary twins*

Masculinity became toxic when love became the last option; Serving was given up for adoption

May the real masculinity please stand up?

Gymnast

I used to be really flexible
Probably one of the only guys that *looked forward*
to
Gymnastics
On the other hand
The masculinity of my peers had been seared
Doctor notes every class to keep them clear

But we all love gymnastics

We all find ourselves splitting in two
As we try to figure out which vice will comfort us
today
Overdose is real
We need to heal
There is comfort in contentment
We don't have to revert to fragments
Everywhere but nowhere

VI: Observations from The Messenger

Zombies

I find zombies fascinating
Dead but somehow living
With brains full of decay they stray
Into impulse

When they lose a limb they still keep crawling in
the same way
Insanity, doing the same thing over and over but
expecting better
Zombies can't think for themselves
Controlled by their senses and stuck in a loop

I find human beings fascinating too
Dead dreams but somehow living
With hearts full of dismay they stray
Into manipulation and mundanity

When they lose a limb they still keep crawling
under the same system
Insanity, doing the same thing over and over but
expecting better
Human beings tend not to think for themselves
Controlled by their senses and stuck in a loop

Maybe we've been making movies about
ourselves all this time?

We Don't Dream

Someone: We don't dream anymore, because as
we grow up our creativity is torn down. Our
imaginations don't work in the real world.
So we've been told.

So,
We chase paychecks and bills paid
Blue ticks and higher pay rates.
It's hard to believe that our minds can birth real
wealth.

"Our imaginations don't work in the real world."
Or at least, we won't explore it long enough to
see
Societal pressures,
The imaginations of others that we have
accepted.
But our own creativity, mind, love and
uniqueness we've neglected.

Saul

Grayscale

You've lost colour in your eyes

On the road to Damascus

Your eyes have gone blind

Zealous policeman

You thought your killing was right...eous

Simulation

What if life was a simulation? What would you do differently? If you had a respawn what would you live for? What if death has already been covered and eternal life was already given? Would you think any differently?

Tell that person you love them, watch their face
fill with glee
Chase your passion, not just see it when you
dream
Make it reality
Because life is really what we make of it
And we can be our worst enemies
What if the people at the top of the world knew
this?
What if they knew that outside of death was not
the end?
So instead, they control us
Through mass outlets, spreading fear,
making us believe that we only have one shot...
"here"

What if life was a simulation? What if you could tune out of the world's station? What if eternal life was already given? What if you could live free outside of the fear of Death's prison?

Maybe you would no longer fear failure
Your daydreams would become real as day
Your nightmares would merely become illusions
of the night
And you wouldn't think twice about living your
most courageous life
What if death could be defeated in your mind?
What if we already had access to eternal life?

Is there something... more?

A Good Friend

A good friend is openly honest
Armed with bullets of rebuke ready to shoot
your heart
So that your dysfunctions finally leak out for
good
A bad friend is subtly deceptive
Often really attractive
Because they look like the embodiment of all the
issues you hold
Attracted to their gossip because you also eat
false stories of others like choice delicacies

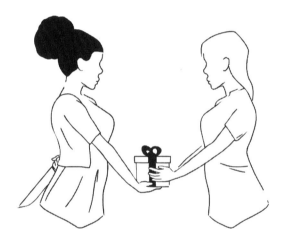

Comfort Zone

I have come to learn
That limits, *though safe*
Are enemies
Lies spoken from mouths
Who love the ground and are scared of the
clouds.
My head was made to reside in the clouds
I was created to fly
Until my feet feel like foreign members
And the touch of the ground is a substitute of
death

...

If the sky's the limit
Why do we fumble our dreams?
Other people who are incapable of flight juggle
our dreams
    They fear that you'll be the one to grow wings
        Leave them behind on the field of green
The comfort zone never belonged to us
It always belonged to them

...

I have come to learn
That limits, *though safe*
Are enemies
Lies spoken from mouths
Who love the ground and are scared of the
clouds

Know Your Rights

Black and white
They say "Know your rights"
What rights?
It's the law we've had to fight
Too many have died

What a shame

Too many to name

My brothers and sisters are being maimed
Modern day slavery is taking place
But I can see the chains will break
I can see the chains will break one day

The Fear of Death

We fear death
More than we fear not living
We should fear not living
More than we fear death

The fear of death is a spider's last breath, laying
on it's back, curling into a ball, as passion crosses
over to the other side
The death you ought to fear: "Was I ever *really
here?*"

You no longer live to be alive
You now live with the fear you'll die
What a big regret
Knowing I wasn't *truly alive* before I died
I no longer fear death
I fear not being alive whilst I have the time

The hamster wheel isn't going anywhere
but time is

it's about time you find you

Passing Time

"I'm   just   p a s s i n g   time"
Time cannot lose in a race
Time is prime, he baffles Usain Bolt; may your
mouth halt from such blasphemy.
Time is an anchor that is slowly dragging
everyone under

Likeness to his first-cousin Gravity
Hyperbolic time chamber X100

He is newborn to child
to adolescent to teenager
to young adult to adult
to middle aged to retired
to elderly to death, the end.
The eternal string that holds all processes
together

He is unforgiving to those who work against him;
Subordination is not in Time's vocabulary
You think you're passing Time but you're passing
behind
"Let's kill some time"
Time doesn't die

You die

Time is an unchanging truth
You'll never kill time
Time is killing you
So will you use Time wisely; will you submit?
Or will your value of Time continue to destroy
you?

A Good Friend #2

Sometimes sparks fly when two friends are
digging into each other's layers
It's not always a bad thing
Full of grace and full of truth
A good friend will make you aware of your flaws,
cover you,
And build you up simultaneously
Good friends tend to carry a list full of
constructive criticism to upgrade your temple
They are great surveyors who foresee future
ruins

A bad friend is an ego-kisser
They seldom want you to know the truth
Such people don't consider the future you
Bad friends are false prophets,
Out of mouths of open graves they state:
"Peace, *all* you do is wonderful"
but eagerly waiting for your self-destructive
tendencies to kill you one day...
Bad friends, never seem to have a bad thing to
say about you.

Check your circle
Judas can be very flattering, almost seductive
The kind of friend that can subliminally
sentence a man to death with a kiss

We tend to have more bad friends than good
Because we would rather be worshipped than
challenged.

This is my generation

It's Rehearsal Time

Sadly our kids won't be the same
Trauma is an understatement
They've been forced to play this game
And now it's rehearsal time again

"When you see a police officer come
Just make sure you don't run
Or he may pull out his gun and..."

They say it was a mistake
It's called murder.

To hate someone because their melanocytes produce a certain amount of melanin is foolish.

Are you foolish? I hope not.

To hate someone because others told you to hate them is the real bondage.

Are *you* really free?

Memory Lane

Now up to your
long-term memory stores.
  Back to when
    you dreamed of
      being independent.
        Remember the days
          when you wanted this?
            You craved to
              leave your cocoon.
                Now you crave
                  for larger wings.
                    Don't let the masses make you
                      forget that you're blessed.
                        Always wanting more is what
                          will make you depressed.
                            When you are content
                              you are at your best.
                                          Slow. Down.

Comfort Is Not for Sale

"Many people lose the small joys in the hope for the big happiness." ~ Pearl S. Buck

I have seen many
Many who spend their money
Seeking comfort
Albeit the noose *still wins* in the end
Elusive is comfort to them

Comfort is not for sale!

Comfort is not tamed by wealth
Where contentment is nurtured
That's where comfort dwells

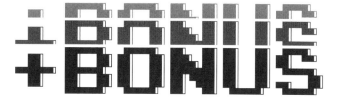

That Time I Had Sensory Overload

What was I doing again?
No. That's not right
I could've sworn that was it?
When did my memory get this bad?
When did information become too vast to
contain for my brain?
Sensory overload, that's her name
Yeah.. What was I talking about again?

Oh yes, sorry sensory overload
My fiance. Closer than a brother, but an enemy
of progress
I can't seem to get rid of her
Blame her for the pauses, forgetfulness, and poor
eye contact...
I'm not uneducated, or bad at English
I've just been captured by her beauty
Peripherals are gone, tunnel vision has switched
on
So, multitasking is a phoenix, a myth

I can't seem to concentrate very well
Because she makes silence sound like a parade
And conversation sound like trumpets
Imagine your hearing being so sharp that you
pick up noises that no one else hears
Imagine your eyes being so sensitive to light that
summer can be a blinding experience
Imagine your skin being so responsive that one
touch feels like a thousand
Even writing this poem is a chore
And speaking in front of you, all the more, a
chore

See no evil. Hear no evil. Speak no evil
Maybe the three wise monkeys had sensory
overload too
I cover my eyes to see no light,
sometimes it's too bright
I cover my ears to hear no sound, because it's like
surround sound all around
I cover my mouth, for I can't stand my broken
English that finds its way to the surface

Remember, I'm not bad at English
My brain just gets stuck sometimes
It's all the over-stimulation in my mind
Overloaded, like a machine that's been
incorrectly coded
How did this start?
I was a nursery teacher for a while
And the over-stimulated environment took its
toll
So my brain started to develop mental holes
The keyhole to my domain was broken so
In came sensory overload and all her baggage

Why did I let her in?
She's a squatter, my door was open and she made
her bed
And she became so much more vicious when I
got the call that my brother was dead
2019, the year this all started
I had so many projects I wanted to release
So many poems I wanted people's minds to eat
I was gonna set a table for a lyrical feast

I'm on a lonely island as if the whole world is
vacant
The world we live in

If they can't see it, they won't believe it
Sensory overload is unseen, only experienced

Enough about me
Precious creative
It's okay if you don't have it all together
When she comes up again to seduce you into
confusion and despair. Take time.
Go outside, get some fresh air.
Affirm yourself with words of care
And try again. Paint again. Sing again. Write
again
Show her who rules your body.
Invisible disabilities only get normalised and
healed,
Depending on how much of your struggle you
reveal

A Tale Called Lockdown

A couple steps for man
A giant leap for mankind
That's honestly how life has felt with us living
inside
The biggest pandemic of our time
What a time to be alive
While the world was at a standstill
I found a deeper me inside
I hope you did too

I hope that you found a new love for nature
Breathed in the sweet air of stillness
And learnt from the trees around us to be patient
Bloom comes from preparation
Allowing old branches that serve no function to
fall
So that new growth may be installed
Make room for updates and upgrades
Because this isn't the end
Don't waste your time wondering because you'll
never get this time again

Spend more time with your family
Check up on all your friends
And as sun rays kiss skin make sure you kiss the
child within
A couple steps for man
A giant leap for mankind
This is your victory lap my friend maximise
your time
Our high tempo normal is coming back
And nature will be hidden again, taken away
from our eyes
Off into the night, the abyss of first world rush,

As you hop into your car for work or run for that
bus

Most of us...
Didn't even realise that Spring went by.
Life isn't running anywhere. We are the ones
running from life
Open your eyes.
Lockdown shouldn't have to teach us twice. Slow
down.

The Fool

Why do they keep leaving?
Maybe my heart contains strings they like to play
with?
Does my heart make beautiful sounds that
escape me?
The sound of strumming
and strings eventually snapping
must sound like music to the ears of those who
leave as they please

Or I'm picking wrong

Maybe I'm choosing to align myself with people
who look like my trauma
But when runaways disguise themselves as
family, friends or fresh lovers—
Can you really blame me?

Before the flags appeared red they were green
A summer dream,
Like an open field of grass
Trees blowing with the wind
People tend to speak your language until autumn
Then the flags turn amber
Leaves change colour
But you are convinced that *it's just the season*
And so you *reason*, you *help*, you *love*, you *fight*
For the green leaves you once gazed upon in the
breeze

Until you realise
They were using your own blood to nourish the
soil underneath them
You were just trying to be a "good friend"

Are red flags always red?
Or are they red in hindsight because of our
blood that's been spilled on them?
My antenna picked up a good signal
Something better than my past abandonments
Who could've known that an EMP
Was waiting for me in the mystery of who these
past people really were

So here's a thought...
When someone says they care about you
Wait
Until their body has learned the rhythm of their
words
Wait
Until love is not just a moment but a living
epistle
Wait
But don't wait too long
Because regardless of how long you wait
Love will always be a risk
And sadly, risk management is not your Saviour
So mitigate but don't negate your feelings, your
love.
Don't be too quick to cover what you see in
others
Let your heart feel
Abandonment is apart of the story
So see the good in people anyway
Abandonment is here to stay

And, to answer your question
Yes, *of course it hurts*
But scars give us a reason to dance and builds
our hearts
So my arms are still open
I am a burgled house still waiting for repairs

My chest, a fragmented door
My shoulder joints are broken hinges

For risking love again and again
Some would call me a fool
I am a fool
But love is reserved for fools

So friend, I know it hurts
But when you get your act together
Your makeup done, and outfit pressed
Here's what is next:

You must risk it all again and again
We lovers can be fools
But love is reserved for fools

VII: The God Letters

"Every letter and word. I heard it all. Audibly and internally. None of this is fabricated. I heard Him, as if we were in the same room. He says I should share some of them, so that He may talk to you too. From my notebook, for your devotion."

These letters are collated from many different times, places and situations.

Ək'septəns|Acceptance

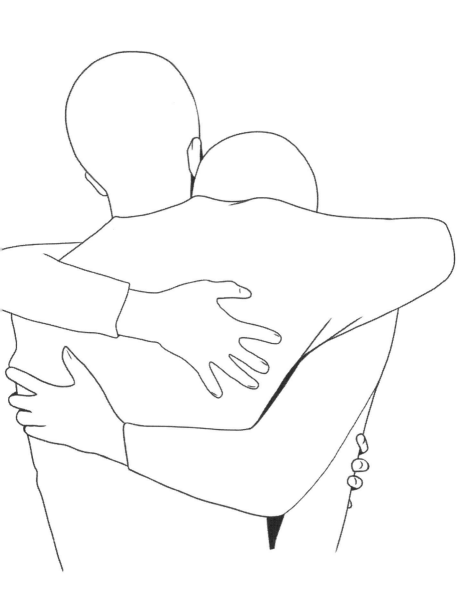

Nothing More, Nothing Less

Let Me deal with you Emmanuel
Come into my presence
Nothing more, nothing less
Give yourself to Me, daily
So I can work on you in good time

You First

Everything I will use you to do for others
I will do it in you first, Emmanuel.

I want you to believe you are fearfully and
wonderfully made despite your supposed
perception of what others think of you.
I want to fully restore the beauty of identity
in you because I will use you to restore the
true identity in others.

Emmanuel, you first.

Believe. Become. Behold.

BELIEVE: You are fearfully and wonderfully made. My death for you proved your value.

BECOME: Begin to walk in this truth by having fellowship with Jesus and My Spirit. Change your vocabulary, look to Me for validation of your image. After all, you are made in My image, so how can you not be beautiful and wonderful?

BEHOLD: The world will see your beauty as you conform to the image of My Son in fellowship with my Spirit, your original blueprint. Others will find confidence in being My image-bearers.

Sonship, again.

Today, you have become My son, and I will become your Father! (Psalms 2:7)
From today onwards you will know sonship like never before!

("Good Good Father" by Chris Tomlin came on shuffle immediately after I heard Him)

Where Can I Go?

Where can I go?

Even after sin you are closer than my skin
You are the air I'm breathing in
You comfort me back to repentance.

*I fell. Again. After promising Him that I
wouldn't. But through the waterfall of tears
drowning my face I saw them... His holy Angels
in my room. Two were seated next to me on either
side, comforting me, hands on my shoulders, also
very tall, their heads towered high.*

You will get what you paid for. Me.
Sin won't stop You.
I cannot get away from You. Even my
darkness is as light to you. You will change
me.

Everything Is Passing

Everything else is passing
Going into the lake of fire
I will only remain, my name is Jesus.
So, only those who remain in Me will not
pass with the earth and heavens.
I am higher than all things
And I invite you to have everlasting life in
Me.

Forsake all other things because they are
passing, and if you are found cemented in
them,
You will pass with them.

My Hype Man

God: "I see a world changer."

*When I stared at a picture of my younger self,
back when I had no clue of the journey before me.
God always saw my future.*

Ōvər'kəm|Overcome

Fire, the Helpful Friend

While you're going through the fire it hurts.
But I have a plan that exceeds what you're going
through right now.
The fire may burn, but it's burning bits that you
don't need.
I will NEVER let it consume you as *long as your
faith is in Me.*
When you are refined as *gold* you will
understand.

I'm with you.
You don't have a brother, friend, King, Father
and God who can't sympathise with your
weaknesses.
Emmanuel,
I've been through it. I overcame. I live inside of
you. You will overcome.
Let's walk through it together. You will
experience resurrection *even as you live.*

Potter and Clay

RECOGNISE I am the Potter and you are the clay,
And with ingredients of dark and light times I
mould you into a strong jar with treasure inside
that cannot be taken.

(As I was writing this I looked up, and the bus
stop we were coming to was called Clay Avenue)

Some of us are being tested, like gold.
Gold is tested so that it doesn't look like a
counterfeit; looking like gold but bending like
plastic is not God's intention for us. God doesn't
want a form of godliness with no substance.

Lord, How?

(After my brother passed and my house burnt
down a month after)
I cried: Lord, how? How will this work out? How
will my life be complete?

....

"You're in My hands.
"Have I ever stopped being your friend?"
No.
"Have I ever stopped loving you?"
No.
"Have I ever stopped partnering with you?"
No.
"Have I ever stopped forgiving you?"
No.
"Have I ever failed you?"
No.
"Have I ever stopped providing for you?"
No.
"Have I ever stopped talking to you for good?"
No.
"Have I ever stopped being your Father?"
... No.

"If it was meant to be over, *I'd have you with Me in
a heartbeat.* I still have new things to do in your
life and through your life," God said softly.

The Burning Bush

I want to turn you into the burning bush.
On fire, but not consumed. A wonder for all to
see.
On fire with trials, but also on fire for Me.
For all to see.

(it is possible to receive the greatest joy you
could ever have through the toughest battles
you've ever fought...)

The Joy of Suffering

I place some of my people on journeys of
suffering so that others won't have to.
The culmination of power gained through
obedience can change others forever
in *one moment*.
I give suffering to those who I consider my
friends.
I give suffering to those who I know will bless
others whilst holding onto Me till the end.
So receive suffering with honour.
For those who suffer in my name will be closer.

I trust you with suffering.

Ləv|Love

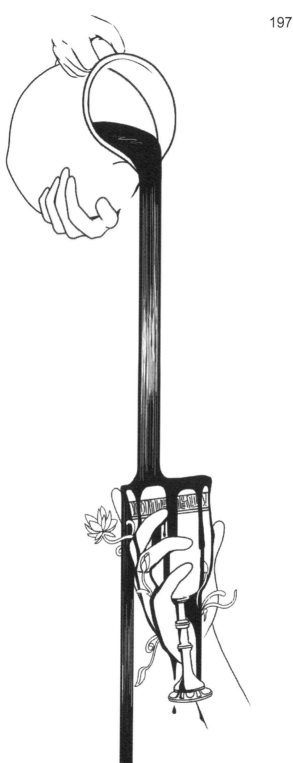

Real Love

Real love sees your future
Real love disciplines you for your future
Real love allows trials to flood around you,
      so you learn how to swim with Me as
      your safety bands
Real love touches the parts you've neglected
by dealing with your past and present
      negatives to develop your *picture*, the
      real you.
Real love makes you uncomfortable to get
      rid of the things you don't need
Real love is Me.

I will change the way you view love.

You're Worth Many Deaths

Believe I love you, believe I died for you.
Believe that I died for you because *you're*
worth dying for.
No human can devalue you if I deemed you
worth a thousand deaths.
My love says you're enough.

AMEN

"AMEN
It *is* finished, and will always be finished
You are mine. You always will be.
My work will *never* be undone.
You are mine forever."

As I lay my head down in the presence of Jesus,
I saw a figure in the Spirit place a robe on my
shoulders and a ring appeared on my finger.
I am reminded by You that I am Yours, just like
the prodigal son.
I have never stopped being Yours no matter how
I've felt on my down days.

Let Love Have the Final Say

God: I give to you, you give to Me.
Me: You give to me, I'll give to You.
God: I give to you, you give to Me.
Me: You give to me, I'll give to You.
God: I give to you, you give to Me.
Me: You give to me, I'll give to You.
God: I give to you, you give to Me.
Me: You give to me, I'll give to You.

~ 1 John 4:19

My Joy

You were a part of the joy set before Me
Crucifixion was palatable because of you

~ Hebrews 12:2

The Spirit Woos

Take My hand and dance with Me.
Forget about what you did, as you dance
with Me.
I have always been with you.
I will always be with you son.
Dance with Me.

If you dance with Me, paying close attention
You'll forget about all your other lovers.

An Invitation

I want to invite you to consider something
As you can see, I've been through a lot.
None of which I could've processed alone
My poems only have the ability to change perceptions
Because someone has consistently been changing my own.
I owe it all to Jesus, my dear friend and confidant.
Here's the best gift I can give to you
Poems are great but He is better.
Open up and let Him read you like a letter
Jesus loves you. Yes you.
And it's okay to come to Him just as you are
You just need a willing heart.
He does the changing
He does the shaping
He does the perfecting.

"Come to Me if you are weary, and I will give you rest"

~ Matthew 11:28

Say this from the depths of your heart;

> "Jesus, I want to know You, so help me to
> know You. I want to know this love that
> changes people for the better. Help me yo
> believe and understand that You died for my
> sins and I have access to eternal life in You if
> I would want it. Heal the painful parts of my
> life. I give myself to you from today
> onwards. I want to be made new. Amen"

Welcome to *the real* poetic persuasion, Jesus.

The one that can turn a young caring,
trauma-filled, depressed, apathetic, hurt,
broken, misunderstood, small and insecure
boy
...into a beloved son.

Acknowledgments

I want to say a big thank you to the First and the Last, the Yes and Amen, the King of kings and the Lord of lords, to my Father in heaven, Jesus Christ and the Holy Spirit for making this all possible. All glory and honour goes to God who strengthens my hands to write.

Shoutout to my biggest supporter, my wife. I am a better man because of you. I want to acknowledge my Mum, Dad and my brothers, as well as all of my cousins, uncles, aunties and grandparents. It takes a village to raise a child, so thank you. I want to specifically shout out my Aunty Stella. You have been God's love in motion to our little family for years, thank you!

I want to acknowledge all of my teachers from Lonesome Primary School and Rutlish Secondary School that shaped my mind in one way or another. Big love to all my Pompey peeps (you know who you are). I want to acknowledge Brixton Topcats Basketball Club, Coach Jimmy Rogers (RIP), Coach Wayne, Coach Nana, Coach Moji, Coach Theo, Coach Jimmy Markham, all of my teammates through the years and others I may be forgetting. You may never know how much of a safe space basketball was for me in my teenage years. Thank you for pushing me, now I can push myself.

Shout out to my SIC family, my accountability lads, my CT church family, my ANT church family, my mentor Tambo and all my friends for continued support, love and prayers over my life, thank you.

... shoutout Ebenezer, FOMO, remember haha.

I want to thank my pastors Ayokunu Oduniyi and Susan Deborahs Oduniyi for their support in my life. I also want to thank all of the other men and women that I may be forgetting for their availability to speak into my life and help me receive guidance when I needed it. I am growing into the summation of the puzzle pieces God placed in all of you. Thank you for your guidance.

Thank you, Jeffrey Osei-Bonsu, for getting me back into poetry and also helping to guide me. None of this may have been possible if it wasn't for your help.

Lastly, but definitely not least, I want to acknowledge Michael Owusu-Kyereh, the illustrator of this book. Every illustration (except for the photos) you see in the pages of this book was done by him. I also want to thank Owen Khang for the book cover sketch. My overseas friend has been kind to me. God bless you.

Fin.

About the Author

Emmanuel Borges-Da-Silva also known as Eman The Messenger is a content creator, fashion designer, poet, poetry script writer, emerging screenwriter, author and unique emerging voice who has several years experience doing commercial, live performance and online poetry/spoken word. Emmanuel has worked with notable organisations such as West Ham United Football Club, Finlandia University Women's Basketball (WBB) and various others.

He is passionate about using spoken word to ignite social justice campaigns, celebrate love (wedding performances), spread wholesome messages through music and much more. Emmanuel would describe his poetry as "poetic persuasion", which simply means to use spoken word poetry to poetically persuade people to change their perceptions for the better. Being a young carer for over 13 years prior to his mother's passing as well as his Christian faith-based background informs his love for change, growth, self-reflection and social justice for all.

Notable work includes, but is not limited to:
- Social Justice Campaign with West Ham United Football Club promoting unity within the football club against racism.
- Poetry script monologue for Finlandia

University WBB in collaboration with Two Mile Media, encouraging the senior players on their season past and their season ahead as they leave the university.
- Poetry Album: The Black Tape
- Multiple bespoke wedding poetry bookings
- 5+ years experience performing live spoken word & poetry.

———--

www.emanthemessenger.com
Instagram: @eman_the_messenger

Business enquiries:
info@emanthemessenger.com

Printed in Great Britain
by Amazon

21017786R00121